no time for fragments

Sermons for Lent

By Karl H. Brevik

AUGSBURG PUBLISHING HOUSE

Minneapolis   Minnesota

NO TIME FOR FRAGMENTS

Copyright © 1970 Augsburg Publishing House

Library of Congress Catalog Card No. 70-101105

Manufactured in the United States of America

To Phyllis, my wife,

whom I love for

a host of

unfragmented reasons

Preface

Christians are invited to live as whole people and to bring healing to a torn and bleeding world. It is incredible that in the face of such need for the words of the Gospel so much precious time is spent in self-examination. Faith in Jesus Christ is more than demanding and clarifying. It makes all of life hang together with meaning and purpose, with joy that floods the spirit.

It is no simple matter to feel and act with honesty in the midst of pressures and fears that break life into abrasive bits. When confidence in Christ is shattered, the comfort of faith retreats. The purpose of these chapters is to pull together some of the fragments of our days. There are many other areas that touch us all, but during this Lenten season look through these chapters for possibilities for healing and wholeness in the Christ who marks all of life with his sign of reconciliation, the cross. Life is short—there is no time for fragments.

Contents

Despite the obvious fact that faith's first assumption is the presence of the living God in the world, it is rare to find a Christian who lives as though he were in the presence of the living God.*

*Henry E. Horn, *The Christian in Modern Style*. Philadelphia: Fortress Press, 1968.

But when the Pharisees heard that he had silenced the Sadducees, they came together. And one of them, a lawyer, asked him a question, to test him. "Teacher, which is the great commandment in the law?" And he said to him, "You shall love the Lord your God with all your heart, and with all your soul, and with all your mind. This is the great and first commandment. And a second is like it, You shall love your neighbor as yourself. On these two commandments depend all the law and the prophets."

Now while the Pharisees were gathered together, Jesus asked them a question, saying, "What do you think of the Christ? Whose son is he?" They said to him, "The son of David." He said to them, "How is it then that David, inspired by the Spirit, calls him Lord, saying,

The Lord said to my Lord,

Sit at my right hand,

till I put thy enemies under thy feet'?

If David thus calls him Lord, how is he his son?" And no one was able to answer him a word, nor from that day did any one dare to ask him any more questions.

Matthew 22:34-46

Chapter One

Handicaps, hardships,

heartaches are shattering - - -

If You Haven't Got It Here

You must love the Lord your God with all your heart, and with all your soul, and with all your mind. Matthew 22:37 (TEV).

Abundant life is the message of the Gospel. Abundant, joy-filled, forward-looking, hopeful life is the message of Jesus Christ, and abundant life is also the message of Lent. This means the ability given by God to relish his gifts in a world twisted and bent by the hostile and fragmenting sins of people, people like you and me. We are to be instruments on which the melody of God's goodness can be played out as we accept his forgiveness and as we love other people.

We live in an age of the church that affects sophisticated self-control and wordy, impersonal theological exercises on the one hand, and lackluster, casual, churchy carelessness and personal dissatisfaction with things as they are on the other. Change is not easy for us because change not only challenges but threatens us. We are easily tempted to allow the rutted patterns of old fears, old frustrations, old guilt, and old disappointments to fragment our days and make us products of disillusionment.

3

If you haven't got it here—and "here" is the point where freshness, beauty, and renewal are discovered, the point where worship comes alive and the capacity for living life is given freely and with releasing power—if you haven't got it here, where those attitudes that make life worth living are fostered, something in your relationship to the living Christ is missing. One of the greatest deterrents to wholeness and happiness, to enjoying the time you have been given is the attitude which always looks on the dark side of things.

This is what makes Lent such a loss for so many. It becomes a weary, dreary, dutiful drag toward Easter. It should be a time of renewal of the things that matter.

Have you allowed yourself to become accustomed to seeing the faults in others rather than their good points; to complaining constantly about your little hardships, rather than being truly grateful for your opportunities; to living in the sad shadows of selfishness, rather than in the bright flash of Christ's light? If your conversation contains more criticism than praise, more disapproval than acceptance, more self-pity than willingness to grow, more whining than laughter, your capacity for the enjoyment of God's gifts is seriously fragmented. It is not a matter of how much time you have, it's how you use it. Lent shows us that life is not meant to be lived in warring fragments but purposefully in the strong name of Jesus Christ.

Begin now to have done with looking for flaws, faults, failures. Start dwelling on forgiveness, opportunities for joy, friendliness, and graciousness, and you will have it in the here and now.

Friends visiting Switzerland went to a chalet high in the

mountains for lunch. Then the father and one of his sons took a walk up one of the rocky paths. Soon they were far above the noise of ordinary things. My friend commented, "It was strange to be in that quiet, beautiful, separated place. I could have stayed for hours just soaking in the solitude."

Worship should be an intensely personal experience, and thus there is something about worship that is almost beyond the adequacy of human language to express. This is one of the reasons I place these familiar words in our parish bulletin each Sunday: "Be thoughtful, be silent, be reverent, for this is the house of God."

Concentration, silence, and reverence are not ordinary characteristics for our hurried, harried days. There are many who laugh at the experience of Peter, James, and John on the Mount of Transfiguration. Standing in the presence of Jesus, all that even the usually verbose Peter could say was, "Lord, it is good for us to be here." But that was all that was necessary. They were glad to have been invited.

When we learn to praise God, our spirits, which are so often disturbed or in distress during the week, are at peace with God. This is what Paul tells us in Romans 5:1:

> Therefore, since we are justified by faith, we have peace with God through our Lord Jesus Christ.

God's attitude is no longer one of stern justice, but of mercy, love, and compassion. The four questions that follow apply to all of us. They speak directly to the fragmentation which afflicts our homes, our parishes, our lives, our society.

They are questions which Lenten awakening seeks to answer:

What do you think of Christ?

The answers of everyone who reads these words will vary widely. In their desire to rid themselves of the troublesome Galilean, those who 1,900 years ago first tried to answer these same questions found their tongues tangled. They, like us, were so embroiled in the problems of religion, or personality, or organization that they forgot to practice what they believed, and missed the joy. It's astonishing how many of us are always attempting to put others to a test to see if they or we measure up. Tests and measurements soon grow both old and cold, as those who put Jesus to the test soon found out. They were unhappy in their religion and were still more unhappy that others had found the joy. Harold E. Kohn has written:

> Religious questions deserve a careful consideration, and an alert and devout mind will continue to seek answers to life's perplexing riddles. But the question is perilous to a person's spiritual welfare if it becomes a substitute for enjoying one's faith.*

What is it that makes one home a place where acceptance and forgiveness are found, where understanding abounds and where harsh judgments are non-existent, and another home stale with festering hostility and nerve-wracking competition?

Our Lord might have said simply that one family had learned to stop testing and start putting love into practice.

---

*Harold E. Kohn, *Thoughts Afield*. Grand Rapids: Wm. B. Eerdmans Publishing Co. Used by permission.

His greatest commandment, after all, was to love God with *all* your heart, *all* your soul, *all* your mind. This came first. Next was to love your neighbor as yourself.

From a personal point of view, on this basis, what do you think of Christ, of his promises, his compassion? Do you believe in his forgiveness, trust him for your salvation, rest in his power to renew and transform? Or have you traded the gift of new birth for nominal membership in an often dull and fragmented church?

When the Pharisees came to Jesus, they were saying in today's idiom, "This guy is really turning people on and we are just the ones to turn him off." They represented the large and unyielding group in the *status quo* oriented institutional church that needed to be jarred loose. Nothing made the Pharisees more irritated, resentful, vindictive than the visible evidence that those who met Jesus Christ had become new people. Nothing makes members of a comfortable club-like congregation of indifferent people more angry than the intrusion of lively witnesses for Christ who are happy in their relationship and do not feel that worship or prayer is either a weary drag or a burden.

We have made it far too simple to be related without commitment to the church as an institution, and because of this we find it convenient to neglect the demands of the Gospel. And we do neglect them, and wonder why we haven't got it here, where the joy and splendor of worship break loose in the family of the faithful.

In writing about the transformation under way in American church life, Robert McAfee Brown has stated frankly that while people on the edges of church life may no longer find comfort in the church, those who remain will know why they have done so.

Harsh? Demanding? Unrealistic? Sure to ruffle the feathers of the careless and the sentimentally inclined? What are those words again? "You shall love the Lord your God with *all* your heart...."

What do you think of yourself?

When *Time* magazine wanted to pick out a program that, in their opinion, was the freshest show on television, they picked Rowan and Martin's "Laugh-In." The magazine's article catches a bit of the frenetic nervousness which goes into this funny, flashy, flamboyant and disconnected program. From "beautiful downtown Burbank" to the smallest hamlet with electricity, "Laugh-In" drives home both satire and corn with a punch. But it's so much, so jarring, so loud and brassy as to easily wear thin. It is a visible expression of the kind of fragmented living that we, in our busy-ness, have produced. Its stars realize this as they ask, "How long can this kind of thing be sustained?" This is a good question for all of us as we look at ourselves. What "Laugh-In" does is dramatize in "sock-it-to-me" fashion a picture of the disconnected life, and it's pointed because in its absurdity there is so much truth.

As you look back over your life what do you think of yourself? Are you able to laugh, to relax, to take a stand, to enjoy other people? Or are you pressed in by fears, so stamped with despair, so bored with inadequacy that you have never seen the real you stand out or up?

Robert A. King has written of the bitter experience of

learning that many adults hide great defeat while still confidently proclaiming a delivering Gospel. Young people begin to discover this when they learn that their parents do not experience the virtues they say are important.

A good point. We are to experience the knowledge of self in the light of Christ's saving Gospel. Sorrow for sin is essential; repentance is somewhat like being skinned alive, but Christ does not leave us bruised and bleeding. He is the Good Shepherd who cares, comforts, heals, and gives us the grace to become what Martin Luther called "whole people."

What do you think of the world around you?

It's a big, confusing place, this world in which we live. So complex and chaotic have its systems and institutions become that many people, knowing neither Christ nor themselves, have become no more than human moles scurrying along the hidden pathways of fear and neglect. When King Solomon dedicated the magnificent temple in Jerusalem, he declared:

> "Behold, heaven . . . cannot contain thee . . . Yet have regard to the prayer of thy servant . . . toward this house . . . of which thou hast said, 'My name shall be there' . . ." (1 Kings 8:27-29).

This is expressed so richly in the phrases:

> O praise the Lord, all ye nations; praise him, all ye people. Alleluia.

This is what Paul was doing when he wrote the congregation in Corinth and told them how thankful he was that

Jesus Christ had enriched their lives with firm and strong faith:

> "It is God himself who called you to share in the life of his son, Jesus Christ our Lord; and God keeps faith."

This is what Carl F. H. Henry meant when he spoke of the need to overthrow the pessimism with which many Christians seem to view the world around them. He said to young Christians everywhere:

> It is time they started to march and sing in the open arena, to lift their voices for Christ with a clarity and courage that our generation failed to muster. Let them carry placards of proclamation, not billboards of condemnation; let them dare to show the dawn rather than merely to damn the darkness.*

Here is a view of the world which is worthy of a child of God, for our lives are to be lived out in the hopeful and spontaneous joy that comes from knowing, in the midst of evil, corruption, and failure, that this is God's world!

What do you think of the future?

Have you tried recently to imagine what life will be like twenty-five years from now, or fifty, or a hundred? The median age in the United States today is twenty-five; 12,500,000 new voters have been added to the rolls since 1964; there are more than 6,700,000 college and university students in America, and a new-born American appears every 14½ seconds. It is toward this kind of future, filled

*Carl F. H. Henry in *Christianity Today,* September, 1968, p. 15. © 1968 Christianity Today, Inc.

with young people alive to the possibilities of tomorrow, that we are moving. But what will we tell them and their generation about Christ that will help them meet their own tomorrows with his help?

Paul said:

> The word I spoke, the Gospel I proclaimed, did not sway you with noble arguments; it carried conviction by spiritual power, so that your faith might be built not upon human wisdom but upon the power of God. 1 Corinthians 2:4, 5 (NEB).

We need a visionary view of the future. Christians and their churches must display the love and generosity that show others we are committed to the cause of Jesus Christ with all that we have and are. This means that for Christians the future is not tomorrow or next year, but here and now. It involves such seemingly simple, ordinary things as caring for each other in compassion and forgiveness, as happy witnessing, as recognizing that the only place to put the mission of Christ is first, as realizing that it isn't necessary to brood over the past, as overthrowing the paralysis of fear of the future, as praying and using the Scriptures regularly, as seeing worship and Holy Communion as something special, as being able to answer the question with which this sermon began: "What do you think of Christ?" with the glad words: "He is my Lord and Savior!"

Now his parents went to Jerusalem every year at the feast of the Passover. And when he was twelve years old, they went up according to custom; and when the feast was ended, as they were returning, the boy Jesus stayed behind in Jerusalem. His parents did not know it, but supposing him to be in the company they went a day's journey, and they sought him among their kinsfolk and acquaintances; and when they did not find him, they returned to Jerusalem, seeking him. After three days they found him in the temple, sitting among the teachers, listening to them and asking them questions; and all who heard him were amazed at his understanding and his answers. And when they saw him they were astonished; and his mother said to him, "Son, why have you treated us so? Behold, your father and I have been looking for you anxiously." And he said to them, "How is it that you sought me? Did you not know that I must be in my Father's house?" And they did not understand the saying which he spoke to them. And he went down with them and came to Nazareth, and was obedient to them; and his mother kept all these things in her heart.

And Jesus increased in wisdom and in stature, and in favor with God and man.

Luke 2:41-52

Chapter Two

From fragmented families
we hear - - -

Parents' Monumental "Why?"

His parents were amazed when they saw him, and his mother said to him, "Son, why did you do this to us? Your father and I have been terribly worried trying to find you!" Luke 2:48 (TEV).

Jesus was a member of a family. With Joseph and Mary and, many believe, his brothers and sisters he lived in Galilee in Nazareth. He was a member of a church. With those of his faith he attended regularly and participated in the feasts, fasts, and customs which made the life of his people significant. Jesus grew to manhood with those who walked the streets and lived in the houses of Nazareth.

One important day for Joseph's family was the journey to Jerusalem for Passover. It was a time for renewing old friendships and making new ones, for worshiping in the temple, for hearing some of the great teachers, and for realizing the strength of faith in God. At the heart of Passover was the promise of blessing, the covenant God made

with Abraham and continued with Isaac and Jacob. Beautiful, colorful, mysterious, and intriguing, the worship led
by the priests was impressive. Luke records how in the
haste of packing to go home, Joseph and Mary thought
that Jesus was with someone else in the group. But he was
not. They found him in the temple sitting among the
teachers, listening to them and asking questions.

"Why?" his parents apparently asked. "Why have you
treated us so?" Perhaps the question is so natural for us
that we have forgotten what it really says. Or perhaps it
reflects so clearly the way we react that it doesn't seem
strange at all. "Why have you done this to us? Now we are
behind and we have been looking frantically for you, and
here you sit. Have you no concern for us? Why?"

Jesus' answer was simply something like this: "Why
were you looking anywhere else? Here is where I must be."
Then they went home to Nazareth. Jesus was an obedient
son. His life was full with the ordinary concerns of growing up. His life was marked by the obedience of a spirit in
tune with the call of the Father to learn, to worship, to
grow.

> And Jesus increased in wisdom and in stature, and in
> favor with God and man (Luke 2:52).

Why did this increase of wisdom and stature and favor
happen to him? Have things changed so in our time that
parents and children, that families, or the family of faith,
are different? There are some stereotypes about family
life that make Jesus' life seem far removed from today.
There is, for example, the Sunday dinner scene in *Life
With Father,* with Papa as the patriarch seated at the head

of the table, very much in charge of the whole situation, and Mama at the other end of the table bowing to the wishes of the head of the house. On either side of the table sit the children, freshly scrubbed, mannerly and dignified. Was it ever really so? There is the picture of Maggie and Jiggs, and of Dagwood and Blondie, with Dagwood as the ineffective fuddle-headed American male who is condescendingly cared for by his so-very-competent wife. Or there is the family in *Peyton Place,* where sex is served like a smorgasbord. Or the Yokums, where the family circle is headed by a matriarch and the males are conveniently emasculated. Many of us know these situations are false, but do we know why?

All of us are part of three families. Each is important and necessary. We are part of the family from which we take our name, we are part of the family of the church, and we are part of the family of mankind. Today as we live in all of these families we are aware of our relationships within each of them. When the Apostle Paul pointed the way to fruitful and satisfying relationships in the many-sided areas of life, he said,

> Do not be conformed to this world, but be transformed by the renewal of your mind, that you may prove what is the will of God, what is good and acceptable and perfect (Romans 12:2).

Think like a Christian, like one who is born anew through the cleansing of Holy Baptism, one who is set free to celebrate being alive, who rejoices in the redeeming grace of God in Jesus Christ, who is obedient to the call to serve his church.

Think like a Christian, in your home with those you know best. Parents are asking many questions today. The gap between what a family is and what a Christian family ought to be is growing all the time. Who is to blame? What can be done?

There are some family pictures that need to be painted clearly. We need handles on which to hang healthy family relationships. There are many non-Christian pictures that need to be erased, for there have been massive changes in family life, much of it difficult and still more the basis of conflict. Armin Grams has written, "To define change it is necessary to know what was and what is."* It is not easy to talk as a Christian at home with those who know you best, unless you are sure of the foundation from which you operate. It is not easy to break habits which make home a hardly bearable hell, and so we must reflect the light of Christ in our relationships with each other.

The question is, how can this be done? We all need to realize that age does not necessarily mean wisdom. Parents, and I am one, need to be alert to the often unhappy truth that their children are reflections of themselves. Parental values, attitudes, language, concerns are transferred to children both in verbal and non-verbal communication. We all need to know this, but some of us are so distracted by other concerns that we do not realize this applies to us. Others are neither anxious nor willing to hear God's Word.

In our home we have a plaque in the entrance hall which reads simply, "Let all guests be received as Christ." When

---

*From *The Christian Encounters Changes in Family Life,* by Armin Grams, copyright 1968. Reproduced by permission of Concordia Publishing House.

I see this, I often think, "Yes, it's true, but members of the family, also!" How?

> —By starting the day with prayer for the members of our family.
>
> —By asking God to give us strength and grace and patience to talk to other members of our family as persons, remembering that anger and sarcasm only breed more of the same.
>
> —By realizing that other members of our family deserve love and forgiveness
>
> —By joyfully sharing the happy times and being strongly supportive during the difficult times.
>
> —By reminding ourselves how Christian obedience renews heart and mind.

These are but a few, but they are a beginning. When Martin Luther saw that the family needed both strength and direction in order to serve Christ as Lord and worship him as Savior, he wrote the *Small Catechism*. It has been translated into English, and as a guide to Christian family life, it still is one of the finest practical summaries of biblical truth ever written. In a sense, it is unfortunate that we teach Confirmation to youngsters when we parents should be taking a refresher course.

Where love and trust and open acceptance exist in a family, communication exists. Where love and trust and open acceptance break down, communication breaks down. Where there is tension, hostility and anger, the family is no longer a family but merely eats in the same house. There is a need for a renewal of the mind, for love and trust and open acceptance of each other, for thinking like Christians at home.

We also must think like Christians at church. Bench marks—a place from which the elevation can be taken and the next path forward can be charted—are important in our lives. We all need permanent places which, in all situations, are solid and sure. The psalmist knew this when he wrote these words:

> Lord, thou hast been our dwelling place in all generations. Before the mountains were brought forth, or ever thou hadst formed the earth and the world, from everlasting to everlasting, thou art God (Psalm 90:1, 2).

Majesty and magnificence, honor and holiness, mystery and wonder are there to overshadow the Christian in his relationship with God. Yet such attitudes often are not reflected. Nor can it be taken for granted that accepting Christ will guarantee that one will have his mind renewed or his spirit lifted. Still we need to think like Christians in church.

Here the effect of thinking with other Christians about the mercy of God, the power of his Gospel, and Christian obedience is enormous. I remember the family who drove one child eighty miles three times a week for private lessons but who were too tired to worship. Or the family who never missed worship but who regarded the effort as meritorious and never really participated. Or the couple who spent their Sunday mornings gossiping and went home wondering why they didn't, as they put it, "get anything out of church."

To think like a Christian it is first necessary to be a

Christian, and this is an act of the grace of God. Luther says it plainly for all of us:

> I believe that I cannot by my own reason or strength believe in my Lord Jesus Christ or come to him, but the Holy Ghost has called me by the Gospel. . . .

To think like a Christian within the family of the church involves some radical mental surgery for a great many people. At the center of life for the family of Joseph and Mary was the temple with the worship and instruction. You cannot think like a Christian in church until you have learned to think like a Christian *about* the church.

There is, for instance, the matter of joyfully giving money to the church. How often do you think about sitting down with your family and talking over the work of your parish and the outreach of world mission, and decide to give up something as a special way of saying "thank you" to God? Many families have been blessed by the goodness of God, their homes filled with expensive furnishings; they have fine food, clothing, recreation, and yet there is no evidence of faith, except, perhaps, a dusty, unused Bible. To think as a Christian in church means to put aside discussion of the church that is petty and lacking either in honesty or perception, and emerge with a new awareness of the power, the potential, and the possibilities latent in the promises of God.

In a special way, we all are following in our Lord's steps when we go to worship. This is a time of high drama when, confronted by God, we are led to honor and obey him. It is in our churches that we discover the love that helps us, in the world around us, to forgive in the name of Christ.

Think as a Christian in every area of your life. The father of several teen-agers said, when he saw an announcement of a sermon on family life, "Boy, Pastor, I hope you lay it on those kids good. What they need is some tough straight talk!" This father would be disappointed if the answer to disjointed and fragmented family life were discipline only. Some conflict, perhaps, is inevitable but when we learn to think as Christians obvious changes begin to take place. Taught by Christ to live, to celebrate, to enjoy, we can be transformed, healed, and made whole. There is no time for broken, fragmented life, either within a family or within the church.

Where do people find you when they come looking for you, as Jesus' parents came seeking him? Do they find you withdrawn behind a shield of self-pity, unable to reach out to others, unwilling to allow others to reach you? Do they find you thinking the worst of others and giving others your worst? Do they find you separated from obedience to God for one of a hundred excuses that are not even worth repeating? Do they find you on a treadmill of money, medicine, boredom, telephone, diets, and neglect of your soul? Do they find you busy doing what is called the work of the church, as long as you are careful not to learn the answer to the "why" of your life? It really doesn't matter. You must determine whether or not you are ready and willing to trust, to receive, and to believe what God has to say as his Gospel reaches into your life. To think as a Christian means to be transformed, to discover the answer to the "why" of life in your family, in the church, and in the world.

"For the kingdom of heaven is like a householder who went out early in the morning to hire laborers for his vineyard. After agreeing with the laborers for a denarius a day, he sent them into his vineyard. And going out about the third hour he saw others standing idle in the market place; and to them he said, 'You go into the vineyard too, and whatever is right I will give you.' So they went. Going out again about the sixth hour and the ninth hour, he did the same. And about the eleventh hour he went out and found others standing; and he said to them, 'Why do you stand here idle all day?' They said to him, 'Because no one has hired us.' He said to them, 'You go into the vineyard too.' And when evening came, the owner of the vineyard said to his steward, 'Call the laborers and pay them their wages, beginning with the last, up to the first.' And when those hired about the eleventh hour came, each of them received a denarius. Now when the first came, they thought they would receive more; but each of them also received a denarius. And on receiving it they grumbled at the householder, saying, 'These last worked only one hour, and you have made them equal to us who have borne the burden of the day and the scorching heat.' But he replied to one of them, 'Friend, I am doing you no wrong; did you not agree with me for a denarius? Take what belongs to you, and go; I choose to give to this last as I give to you. Am I not allowed to do what I choose with what belongs to me? Or do you begrudge my generosity?' So the last will be first, and the first last."

Matthew 20:1-16

Chapter Three

In a greedy world
we need to know that - - -

God Is a Spendthrift.

"Don't I have the right to do as I wish with my own money?" Matthew 20:1-16 (TEV).

We may not have trouble remembering the goodness of God and the wonder of his grace. But God also is a spendthrift, and this is a concept which can captivate the mind, enlarge the spirit, and open doors to what it means to be a child of God. His spendthrift generosity can be seen in the craggy peaks of the Himalayas jutting against the blue of the sky; in a gently waving field of North Dakota wheat; in a Montana sunset; in a summer evening beside a Minnesota lake. This goodness of God's should infect you, too, with an understanding of his generosity so that you also will become a spendthrift. Many of us are convinced that, in our unique situations, the promises of God cannot help us. Verses like those in Matthew 20 reveal the conviction of Jesus concerning the central truth of his life and ours. God is a spendthrift. Because of our

Puritan heritage, that statement is uncomfortably unsettling. Yet, even the Gospels testify to the fact that God is a spendthrift. And in the Old Testament we read that when Solomon offered his majestic prayer of dedication for the temple, the glory of the Lord filled the Lord's house:

> When all the children of Israel saw the fire come down and the glory of the Lord upon the temple, they bowed down with their faces to the earth on the pavement, and worshiped and gave thanks to the Lord, saying,
>
> > "For he is good,
> > for his steadfast love endures for ever."
> >
> > 2 Chronicles 7:3.

There was a breakthrough at the temple dedication of God's glory, goodness, and steadfast love, and when it came, the people bowed down, worshiped him, and gave thanks to the Lord who had made a covenant of love with them. Throughout Scripture the breakthrough of the "spendthrift" God is seen in his dealings with people. He is the Lord, the Creator, the King who, in Jesus Christ, has poured out all that we might know him as Savior and Lord.

The editor of *Punch,* the English humor magazine, was a guest on the TV "Today" program. He said that, in his view, there was a lack of ability to see the humor in the absurdities and vanities of human life. Looking about America, he saw a tense kind of forced, sick humor that was jibing and cruel. As I went through the day, I saw abundant evidence of the truth of his observation—expressions of hopelessness, sourness, dejection, and bewilderment.

To explain God's spendthrift joy, Jesus used a parable about laborers in the vineyard. To understand this parable, it is essential to see God as the Lord, the Sovereign, the Householder, calling us by his grace into his employ. To participate in the working out of God's plan for life is to be a part of eternal life. *This means that all men are dependent upon the grace of God.* In this parable Jesus makes the point that only those who realize God's mercy are able to see the foolishness and the absurdity of those who begrudge God his generosity.

Jesus also knew the obsession of people with money, so he spoke frequently about money, the spending of it, the saving of it, and where real treasure lies. This text is so pertinent that it is almost painful.

Speaking of a successful but unhappy couple, this comment was made: "I just don't understand it. They have everything that money can buy." The implication was clear; they had nothing, except money.

On our coins there is a simple but subtly deceptive phrase: "In God we trust." *Do we,* really?

Viewing a majestic church building, this angry comment was made: "Such extravagance. Where will it all stop?"

Within the church there is no subject which raises temperatures and turns people off as quickly as money. Perhaps this is the reason we need to hear the message of this parable, which is not about money but about relationships, employment, and generosity. We have all read articles telling us that we are a nation living on credit. We see the ads that invite us to get rid of our debts by borrowing more money, and we are more ready to feel caught in a web of circumstance than we are to see our place in the scheme of things.

In his column in the *Chicago Daily News,* Sidney Harris wrote that the question most often asked him as a columnist was how he found something to write about every day. His answer was that in a world so full of fascinating things, the problem was not how to find something to write about, but how to limit himself to a single subject. There was such an abundance of new, fresh, fascinating, different ideas.

Every person needs to have his life filled with helpful, satisfying, and productive work. This means being wanted, being regarded as useful and valuable, being recognized as having worth. The most unhappy people I see as a pastor are those who have no sense of the great gifts of God which are shared as relationships are shared. In Jesus' parable there is a question which is asked of us all concerning our relationships with others: "Why do you stand here idle all day?" The phrase "laborers for his vineyard" may tune out many of us today, but it should not because we all are called by God to effective and meaningful work in his vineyard.

Goldie Bates was 82 when she came in for adult instruction. Never baptized, she was received into the church by means of this sacrament. Her witness to others was magnetic. "Did you know I was baptized and I am a member of the church?" she would ask, as her eyes twinkled with warmth and good humor. Her conversation was liberally salted with references to what Christ and the church meant to her. She died at 85, and after her funeral at least a dozen people came to tell me she had inspired them to learn what being a Christian was all about. Goldie was a spendthrift for God and, though she discovered late in life what it meant to be a laborer in the vineyard, she was happy because she did.

What about you? Why do you stand idle all day? Can you answer, "Because no one has hired us," as did those in the parable?

After a conversation in which a church member had expressed anger and hostility, a listener asked, "What ever happened to her Christianity?" To which someone else replied, "Did she ever really have any?" A good question. In her anger she displayed what we all tend to display at times—excessive spending of energy and emotion on anger and jealousy. We become spendthrifts with the poison of pettyness, the sickness of selfishness, and the bickering of bitterness. We are unhappy with God because of his generosity—a contradiction and yet true. We are unable to give others the joy, the support, the warmth they need, because our own floodgates are stopped. What ever happened to *your* Christianity? Or did you ever really have any?

We must be alive to the generosity of Christ. If we hoard his gifts, we will never know their joy. So John Bunyan could write:

A man there was, and they called him mad
the more he gave, the more he had . . . .

In the cold, piercing, calculating light of day, nothing seems more irrational than the message of this parable. Jesus' parable tells us that, with God, those who enter early are blessed and those who enter late are blessed also, and there is no place for complaint, criticism, jealousy, or comparison. Each one is given the privilege of exercising fully and without fear the gifts he has in the work of the kingdom. And the work and relationships a Christian enters into are good and gracious gifts of God, a spend-thrift God. Think what this means to you, for you, too, are called to be a spendthrift. Congregations of spendthrifts is what we are called to be as we learn how to use the gifts of God with openness and abandon.

Where is the vineyard into which you are called? Is it where you are, although this may not be where you want to be? But it is here you are to learn to be an extravagant person, overflowing with the warmth and the kindness that stems from the Spirit.

> Let all bitterness and wrath and anger and clamor and slander be put away from you, with all malice, and be kind to one another, tenderhearted, forgiving one another, as God in Christ forgave you (Ephesians 4:31, 32).

These are to be spent, squandered: kindness, tender-heartedness, forgiveness. There is no need to stand idly by and contemplating our difficulties. We can listen to God tell us to go into the vineyard, too. There is joy, release, and satisfaction in realizing that God has a place for us. Jesus' message is that Lent can be the time, the place, the op-portunity to learn to become a spendthrift for him.

Your life, like mine, is largely ordered by what we say to ourselves and by what others say to us. This is the reason we need to hear what God has to say so we can repeat it in word and action in the days ahead. God's word is God's power for us, not weak words of failure which sap strength, steal joy, undermine hope, and cause spiritual anemia. These strong, healing, invigorating words speak of the power of the living Lord in our lives:

> - - - you are to think of yourselves as dead to sin but alive to God in union with Christ Jesus (Romans 6:11 TEV).

> - - - you have been cleansed from sin; you have been dedicated to God; you have been put right with God through the name of the Lord Jesus Christ and by the Spirit of our God (1 Corinthians 6:11 TEV).

> - - - be joyful always, pray at all times, be thankful in all circumstances. This is what God wants of you, in your life in Christ Jesus (1 Thessalonians 5:16-18 TEV).

> - - - freedom is what we have—Christ has set us free! Stand, then, as free men, and do not allow yourselves to become slaves again (Galatians 5:1 TEV).

> - - - so then, as often as we have the chance we should do good to everyone, but especially to those who belong to the family in the faith (Galatians 6:10 TEV).

> - - - do not lose your courage, then, for it brings with it a great reward. You need to be patient, in order to do the will of God and receive what he promises (Hebrews 10:35, 36 TEV).

> - - - there is nothing in all creation that will ever be able to separate us from the love of God which is ours through Christ Jesus our Lord (Romans 8:39 TEV).

Strong words! Some may say that they have been snatched out of their proper context. Then read them in the proper context and discover even more of the way that Jesus Christ continues to come with positive productive power into the lives of those who with willing honesty receive his spendthrift grace.

Yes, God is a spendthrift. The cross and the resurrection tell us this, and so does this text. We are to be spendthrifts, too—mirrors of the grace of God as we are called into the vineyard. There is a beautiful description by Tennyson of King Arthur coming to the Round Table, where his knights are seated. Tennyson wrote:

> I beheld
> From eye to eye thro' all their order flash
> a momentary likeness of the King.

This is what the generosity of a God and Savior will do for us—create a likeness, not momentary but lasting, of the King. Start today to be a spendthrift. Don't hold back; allow the likeness of Christ to shine through so that the light of his generosity may be seen clearly in you. God is a spendthrift, and you can be one, too.

Now he was casting out a demon that was dumb; when the demon had gone out, the dumb man spoke, and the people marveled. But some of them said, "He casts out demons by Be-elzebul, the prince of demons"; while others, to test him, sought from him a sign from heaven. But he, knowing their thoughts, said to them, "Every kingdom divided against itself is laid waste, and house falls upon house. And if Satan also is divided against himself, how will his kingdom stand? For you say that I cast out demons by Be-elzebul. And if I cast out demons by Be-elzebul, by whom do your sons cast them out? Therefore they shall be your judges. But if it is by the finger of God that I cast out demons, then the kingdom of God has come upon you. When a strong man, fully armed, guards his own palace, his goods are in peace; but when one stronger than he assails him and overcomes him, he takes away his armor in which he trusted, and divides his spoil. He who is not with me is against me, and he who does not gather with me scatters.

"When the unclean spirit has gone out of a man, he passes through waterless places seeking rest; and finding none he says, 'I will return to my house from which I came.' And when he comes he finds it swept and put in order. Then he goes and brings seven other spirits more evil than himself, and they enter and dwell there; and the last state of that man becomes worse than the first."

As he said this, a woman in the crowd raised her voice and said to him, "Blessed is the womb that bore you, and the breasts that you sucked!" But he said, "Blessed rather are those who hear the word of God and keep it!"

Luke 11:14-28

Chapter Four

When rough times hit,
we learn what it's like to - - -

Live Through the Drought

"When an evil spirit goes out of man, it travels over dry country looking for a place to rest; if it doesn't find one, it says to itself, 'I will go back to my house which I left!'" Luke 11:24 (TEV).

> O God, let us this day not dull what you have made bright and sparkling clear, let us not empty with carelessness that which you have filled with joy, let us not waste with ease what you died to give in abundance. Into the restless dryness of our lives come now with the life-growing freshening of your power and pierce us awake, that as we have your word spoken to us, we may speak your life to one another. In the name of Christ the refresher. Amen.

A memory from my Navy days that often floods my mind is the experience of sitting alone after a late watch as the ship cut a path through the cold beauty of the lonely sea. As the phosphorescent bubbles left a seemingly endless wake and the stars appeared to be so close that an outstretched hand could bring a handful to earth, a sense of repose and wonder often came. With water all around, there was a feeling of both unity and separation from the cares and ills of the world.

Jesus spoke of the danger and the opportunity of being a Christian. To experience the healing of the Gospel is the beginning of life in Christ. Yet it is at this point the spirits of division enter and make their home in the place Christ has cleansed and set in order. Let us examine how to live through the drought and what Christ saw as needed to water the dry spots of life.

Water always has had a compelling attraction for people. A caravan winding across the desert and stopping at the oasis presents a picture with which we all can identify. Those who remember the great droughts of the 1930's, when windows were taped against the sand and trees were stripped of their leaves by driving wind, also remember the eerie atmosphere associated with familiar watering places gone dry.

Restlessness and anxiety were much in evidence and the real character of people was seen as the dry, hot, dusty, abrasive weather continued. In a living death, the fruits of the earth were robbed of fulfillment because there was no water.

When the rain came, what a miraculous change it brought as parched land and parched lives together drank deeply, and the reality of the dependence of each upon the other came through in gentle life-giving rain. Life had purpose and meaning, and the anxiety and irritation were washed away. Then, all too suddenly, the gratitude and the spirit of wonder were washed away, too, and life was as usual, with its same old divisions.

It's not pleasant to live through a drought, particularly when you feel that you have your house pretty well in order and your life quite well arranged. Jesus declared that we must fill our lives with the fruits of the Holy Spirit, which are refreshing, recreating, invigorating. We all need to be alert to the truth that spiritual housecleaning is a daily necessity. Does that sound like pious claptrap? Nonetheless, it is a fact. When the Apostle Paul spoke of the fruits of the Spirit, he was speaking of the gifts of the Holy Spirit. He said:

> But the fruit of the Spirit is love, joy, peace, patience, kindness, goodness, faithfulness, gentleness, self-control; against such there is no law (Galatians 5:22, 23).

These are the fruits which should inhabit the rooms of your spiritual house daily. Sir William Osler spoke of "living in day-tight compartments." He said: "Throw away all ambition beyond that of doing the day's work well. Live neither in the past nor in the future, but let each day absorb your entire energies and satisfy your wildest ambition."*

Remember, this is a daily matter. One of the most misleading teachings that has ever involved Christian lives is, sadly, as prevalent now as ever. This is the thinking which says, in effect, "After I get myself in shape by straightening out my life, by manicuring my soul, by being good, and by pulling my morals into shape, then . . . ." All this does

---

*Leonard Griffith, *God's Time and Ours*. Nashville: Abingdon Press, 1964.

is make, as Jesus reminds us, the last state worse than the first.

Putting your spiritual house in order is something you cannot do. The miracle of new birth is far greater than that of physical birth, for it is in truth a rebirth, the ultimate reason for being. This comes about as you open yourself to the cleansing and renewing of the Holy Spirit who, when welcomed, produces for you the fruits of the new life in Christ as naturally as a healthy tree produces fruit.

This does not always happen because we shun the needed housecleaning. John said that we love darkness rather than light, but God is light, not darkness. We need to pray:

> Breathe on me, Breath of God;
> Fill me with life anew,
> That I may love what Thou dost love,
> And do what Thou wouldst do.   SBH, 470.

Lent is an excellent time for us to do some personal checking on our spiritual housecleaning.

This Gospel is also a reminder of the fact that all of us are incurable collectors. We collect relationships with which we feel safe and comfortable, and which do not threaten us. This can be truly helpful in the midst of difficulties. But comfortable collectivitis can also be an infection in family life, in the congregation, in our vocation, and in our neighborhood. We tend to become attached to those people who will neither make demands upon us nor encourage change in us. For many the best word picture of the Gospel describes it as a gentle fall of rain which waters the parched places and brings forth growth. Growth means change—not a casting off of the roots of the past, but a stretching toward the future.

What are you collecting? An insatiable desire for things, an overriding appetite for money is a sickness. A fear of being discovered that makes you hang on to falsity can mean that you are dried up, that your spiritual muscles are atrophied.

H. G. Wells once called people who, when they were not going somewhere or coming back from somewhere, the "Godsakers." They were always exclaiming, "For God's sake, let's do something." In the schools, the church, the community, the synod, the political arena, this is the dry, useless plaint that seems to arise when evil spirits come trouping in. A man recently died in New Haven, Connecticut. He had been born and lived all his life in the same room in which he died. The newspaper account of his death said he never had slept in any other room. He had collected what many people have—a severe case of self-absorption. This is the other side of the coin, but neither constant running about nor shutting ourselves up is the answer to living through the drought.

It was Jesus' wish for each of us and for his church that we live in the recognition of both the danger and the possibility of the present moment. Some of you may remember a tragedy some years ago in Jackson, California, when forty-seven miners were entombed in a gold mine. Every effort was made to get them out, but when the diggers finally got through they were dead. Shut up in one of the richest rooms in the world, they literally gasped their lives away. That gold was of no value without the breath of life.

Ernest Gordon wrote of the miracle of faith as it came to the men in the famed Japanese prison camp on the River Kwai:

> Ours was the Church of the Spirit, it was a throbbing heart which gave life to the camp and transformed it in considerable measure from a mass of frightened individuals into a community. From it we received the inspiration that made life possible. Such inspiration was not merely a rosy glow in the abdomen, but the literal inbreathing of the Holy Spirit that enabled men to live nobler lives, to become kind neighbors, to create improvements for the good of others. . . . The fruits of the Holy Spirit were clearly in abundance.*

Here were men in prison who were free, truly and spiritually free. On the membership rolls of Jesus Christ's church are many who are free to move about but who are figuratively bound and imprisoned. The answer is not smooth words, not comforting, flattering, or dishonest attention to selfishness for fear of offense. The answer is the Gospel which says that those who are "in prison" can be free because of the Word of Jesus Christ; that if grace can make us free, we will be free indeed.

This is the word of hope for the dry places, the answer to how to live through the drought.

---

*Ernest Gordon, *Through the Valley of the Kwai*. New York: Harper & Row, Publishers, Incorporated, 1962.

Moses said to the Lord, "See, thou sayest to me, 'Bring up this people'; but thou hast not let me know whom thou wilt send with me. Yet thou hast said, 'I know you by name, and you have also found favor in my sight.' Now therefore, I pray thee, if I have found favor in thy sight, show me now thy ways, that I may know thee and find favor in thy sight. Consider too that this nation is thy people." And he said, "My presence will go with you, and I will give you rest." And he said to him, "If thy presence will not go with me, do not carry us up from here. For how shall it be known that I have found favor in thy sight, I and thy people? Is it not in thy going with us, so that we are distinct, I and thy people, from all other people that are upon the face of the earth?"

And the Lord said to Moses, "This very thing that you have spoken I will do; for you have found favor in my sight, and I know you by name." Moses said, "I pray thee, show me thy glory." And he said, "I will make all my goodness pass before you, and will proclaim before you my name 'The Lord'; and I will be gracious to whom I will be gracious, and will show mercy on whom I shall show mercy. But," he said, "you cannot see my face; for man shall not see me and live." And the Lord said, "Behold, there is a place by me where you shall stand upon the rock; and while my glory passes by I will put you in a cleft of the rock, and I will cover you with my hand until I have passed by; then I will take away my hand, and you shall see my back; but my face shall not be seen."

Exodus 33:12-23

Chapter Five

An amazing responsiveness
comes when we realize - - -

Faith Is No Easy Matter

". . . if I have found favor in thy sight, show me now thy ways, that I may know thee and find favor in thy sight." Exodus 33:13.

Faith was no easy matter for Moses, it was no easy matter for the disciples, and it is no easy matter for you or me. Christian life is a matter of faith in action or of faith active in love. Religious life cannot be separated from the history of which we all are a part. To be a person, a whole person trusting in the promises of God, is to have the gift of faith. When knowledge, assent, and trust are applied, faith can come to life in a personal way. We do not naturally trust or follow; we doubt and balk. Promises to be fulfilled in the future are laid aside by the pressing needs of the present. To believe in God, in his Gospel, in Jesus Christ, is to have confidence that what God says in Scripture is true, and this is not an easy matter.

There is a delightful cartoon that points out what

faith does to a person. A man is shown at a counter in a bookstore. There are stacks of religious books, all with titles about peace and rest and comfort and the easy way. The man is saying to the bookseller, "Have you got something that won't give me cow-like complacency about the world? I want to be aroused, stimulated, stirred."

Gone is the idea that faith is easy or restful. Comforting and assuring, absolutely! But easy, never!

Faith in Christ is stimulating. When the church loses its Christian flavor, and membership becomes flaccid, it has lost its toughness of character. Heroes of the faith never were called into a family of followers so frightened of their own shadow that they never did anything more daring than take a stand on the time of day, and then only after checking.

Halford Luccock wrote of a man who described an acquaintance by saying, "He's as insipid as the white of an egg."* Perhaps we all would agree that there are few things that excite us as little as the white of an egg. Yet there are those who want unexciting religion, who want a preacher who dispenses bromidic platitudes and who want the demands of the Gospel diluted to the point of neutrality.

But platitudes have nothing to do with faith that lives, that brings about growth and maturity through Christ. Platitudes have never brought anything but a false sense of relief to you or to me. Spouting religious platitudes actually is sidestepping involvement in issues, some of them

---

Halford Luccock Treasury. Nashville: Abingdon Press.

controversial, on which the church must speak out, and clearly.

Faith is not a matter of easy evasion of the essential elements of life for which Jesus died, and thus faith in him is no easy matter. We often expect faith to operate on our terms. You know the story of the harried order boy in the grocery store who hung up the phone and sighed wearily. When asked what was the matter, he said, "She wants this order delivered yesterday." Impatience strikes again!

Moses had seen God's mighty acts for the children of Israel, but he wanted even more assurance. He said to God what we so often say, with an arrogance that is terrifying and in words something like these: "If you are not willing to give me what I want, just leave me alone and don't expect any more faithfulness from me. Don't you realize how distinct my contribution has been and how unique my situation is?" Moses wanted God to reveal himself, and he also wanted a vantage point from which to see his character, his glory. He was not satisfied with what God saw fit to disclose; he wanted more, a great deal more.

We should not underestimate, however, Moses' recognition of the leadership of God. Never do we hear him wailing about adversity, or how tough life is, or how he is expected to give God his total allegiance; he did not sit back and tell God how things should be going. Rather, he was so close and so involved that he wanted an even deeper revelation of the activity of God in his life and in the history of his people. We see no evidence of his becoming so preoccupied with petty material pleasures that there was no room left for the eternal. We are not all like Moses. Paul put this well in Romans 12:16 (KJV) when he said, "Be not wise in your own conceits."

Paul's point was clear. God does not operate outside a personal-historical context. He operates where you live, not on your terms, but on the basis of what he has done and promises to do. This is what we call faith and trust, and they issue not from stubborn recalcitrance but from willing obedience. Secondly, for Moses or any of the other people met in Scripture there were only two options: They could stay where they were, or follow in faith. This is true for all of us. Lent, for some, is a sweet sinking into the swamp of sentimentality. This stinks of self-indulgence. Each year Lent calls many to such sad and serious introspection that the difficult joy of moving out of old ruts is never realized. Moses had a difficult assignment; he wanted some assurance before he undertook another mission for God. The woman from Canaan followed after Jesus, although she could have stayed home and fretted about how God was treating her and why her friends were able to get by without trouble.

There is no life without burdens. It has been my observation that those who have the least to worry about and who have the greatest blessings in the realm of material things do the most complaining. Complaint is a cancerous sickness which destroys any joyous relationships with other people and the world. Complaint fragments conversations and relationships into pieces of unhappy hurts. And why?

Emily Bronte, author of *Wuthering Heights*, lived and wrote in a rectory on the bleak, gray moors of Yorkshire.

She spent her days with her half-demented father, two sisters dying from tuberculosis, and a brother who regularly came home howling drunk from the village tavern. Yet she could write:

> No coward soul is mine.
> No trembler in world's storm-troubled sphere;
> I see Heaven's glories shine,
> And faith shines equal, arming me from fear.*

She could have done nothing but complain about her situation, but she had faith and a sense of the eternal which gave dimension and direction to her short life. This is what faith should mean to us today. Do you want to stay as you are, or are you willing to trust?

Thirdly, we need to be so conscious of the power of God that we realize that he has declared all we need to see or know. A few days ago a man told me that he didn't like to be tied down to any responsibilities to the church because of his weekend interests. Not long after that, a woman told me that she thought the requirements for confirmation should be relaxed because her child didn't like to be tied down to things. I saw in both these people a lack of dedication and commitment and trust.

We all need to be reminded that we are called, not to a Sunday morning brunch, but into the company of the redeemed where enlistment is on the terms of Jesus and his Gospel. We do not need a palatable, easy, attractive, socially acceptable kind of arrangement which allows us to decide whether or not the demands are too stringent. We need to be tied down to the fundamentals of the faith. We need to

---

*Halford Luccock Treasury. Nashville: Abingdon Press.

hear again and again that we are followers of Christ who was nailed to the cross for the sake of wishy-washy, easily distracted, self-pitying, thin-skinned, self-righteous people like you and me.

When we follow in faith the way God has prepared we discover many sorts of surprises. This was true for Moses, it was true for the early Christians, and it is true for us. Christian life and faith are not the result of arguments, but of surprises. Those who think their mental gymnastics will impress you will awaken rudely to the fact that they have been called to trust him. Jesus Christ is faith, and faith is Jesus Christ. Devotion to him and trust in him bear fruit as we do our duty through days of drabness, discontent, disillusionment, defeat, discouragement. It is during those times when faith is no easy matter that we encounter the surprises of the Gospel.

We often fear surprises, even though we look forward to them. The gift of Christ may be such a surprise that his offer of forgiveness, renewal, and joy may shake us to our very foundations. Yet it is the glory of the Christian faith that Christ brings into our lives new power for action. Do we want this power?

"And her daughter was made whole from that very hour." She became a new person. So can we, by the gift of faith. "Therefore, if any man is in Christ, he is a new creation" (2 Corinthians 5:17). "Behold, I stand at the door and knock; if any one hears my voice and opens the door, I will come in . . ." (Revelation 3:20).

Perhaps faith on God's terms has more joy and surprises than difficulties and barriers. He promises that this joy, these surprises are waiting for us.

After this Jesus went to the other side of the Sea of Galilee, which is the Sea of Tiberias. And a multitude followed him, because they saw the signs which he did on those who were diseased. Jesus went up into the hills, and there sat down with his disciples. Now the Passover, the feast of the Jews, was at hand. Lifting up his eyes, then, and seeing that a multitude was coming to him, Jesus said to Philip, "How are we to buy bread, so that these people may eat?" This he said to test him, for he himself knew what he would do. Philip answered him, "Two hundred denarii would not buy enough bread for each of them to get a little." One of his disciples, Andrew, Simon Peter's brother, said to him, "There is a lad here who has five barley loaves and two fish; but what are they among so many?" Jesus said, "Make the people sit down." Now there was much grass in the place; so the men sat down, in number about five thousand. Jesus then took the loaves, and when he had given thanks, he distributed them to those who were seated; so also the fish, as much as they wanted. And when they had eaten their fill, he told his disciples, "Gather up the fragments left over, that nothing may be lost." So they gathered them up and filled twelve baskets with fragments from the five barley loaves, left by those who had eaten. When the people saw the sign which he had done, they said, "This is indeed the prophet who is to come into the world!"

Perceiving then that they were about to come and take him by force to make him king, Jesus withdrew again to the hills by himself.

John 6:1-15

Chapter Six

If faith is fragmented,
we need to ask - - -

Are We Prepared?

". . . pick up the pieces left over; let us not waste a bit."
John 6:12 (TEV).

Many complexities disrupt our attempts to meet what each new day brings. Casting about for certainty, we seem more often confused than prepared.

Three words—faith, preparation, and attitude—bring this word from John into perspective. The Gospel deals with God's promises as they are fulfilled in Christ the Savior who came to the first disciples and who comes to you and to me and says, "Follow me."

The miracle of the multiplication of the bread and the fish is a wonderful story, a delight to read and to apply to our lives and work. Preparation is important. So is attitude, whether it is a student getting ready for an exam, a couple planning for marriage, a pastor working on a sermon, a gardener checking seeds before planting, a salesman as he is approaching his first call of the day, a family getting ready for Sunday worship. Preparation is important, not for the task alone but to set the stage for accomplishing what is intended. In preparation, attitude is fundamental because your attitude will determine almost entirely the experiences you have. Not that attitude is the answer. W. Clement Stone, of Evanston, Illinois, one of America's richest men, has parlayed preparation and a positive mental attitude into a third of a billion dollars. So for him these things seem to have worked but, of course, he worked too.

What about all the other people—and you may be one of them—those who with diligence and loyalty struggle and try and seem to run into one obstacle after another? What about those who lust after the keen flavor of success and find that dreams are dashed to dullness and only fragments remain? What about those for whom every day seems to be no more than another serving of yesterday's bitter leftovers? What part does preparation for something better or different or an attitude of understanding play in their lives or in yours or mine?

Jesus often made it pointedly clear that it is possible to get so wound up in preparation for what we think we are going to enjoy that the possibilities in what we often regard as ordinary, daily, routine, and monotonous are forgotten. When this happens in any life it is up to someone else to add some flavor to the daily round. How we look at what we are actually doing tells much about what we are preparing for as the pattern of our days evolves. It's a simple matter to construct a skin-deep veneer of interest in things that matter and all the while leave someone else to carry through, to get the job done. This can be seen in the way we bustle about. Richard C. Cabot has said that for many Christians Paul's pungent "This one thing I do," has become, "These forty things I dabble in."

Let's face it. There is no such thing as an ideal situation, a place without pressing problems, a life without pain, a family without stress and irritation, a parish where there is no need for growth in maturity, shared hospitality, and graciousness. All this means is that there is nowhere, absolutely nowhere, where the ordinary daily necessities can be left undone. Someone must share in the acts that make life bearable. Too general? Perhaps. But when we learn by the grace of Christ to try to understand, rather than to shatter with lack of attention what is essential, a fresh awareness of preparation is born. We all must be involved in a host of tasks that we would rather leave undone.

For the past several years we have witnessed a rash of what is delicately called "protests" on campus after campus. That there is much that needs protesting in our universities is a commonplace observation. But when a handful of irrational adolescents with little insight and less experience "occupy" buildings and ransack offices, what happens? An army of newspaper men and mobile television units materialize to capture for posterity the immortal words of the protestors. When it is all over and the demands for amnesty and total student participation in the planning of curriculum and administration of the university have been made, the cleanup takes place. Then the broken windows are replaced, the refuse picked up and the garbage hauled away—by someone else.

Some of these protesting young people are highly intelligent and competent. They are asking questions and demanding answers. They are forcing a re-evaluation of much in our society that has been regarded as axiomatic. Hopefully they will recognize that the work of the everyday world goes on even as those who drop out of the Establishment look on. Before we fault them, though, let us remember that this kind of attitude can be expanded into many areas, some of which hit close to home—your family, your parish, or your community. Complaint without constructive involvement is valueless and a shallow sham.

De Quincy, the British author who turned on with narcotics long before today's wave of users, never cleaned up the rooms in which he lived. When he could no longer bear the mess, the clutter, and the confusion, he would find another place to live. Someone else always had to come in and clean up the chaos he left behind.

Every once in a while, no matter how we attempt to hide it, we all would like to drop out, to leave everything and get away. But there is more than leaving that matters. Putting the pieces of the puzzle in place is really what Lent is about, at least partly. And dropping out into defeat or despair or anger has never answered anything.

Wrestling with the need for positive and constructive changes in the means used to make God's message known to men strains many relationships. There has been a strange concert of voices, not always melodious, telling the need for change in the way things are done in the local parish. Perhaps you saw the protest bumper sticker that read "The A.B.M. is an Edsel." When I read some of the critics of the parish church and her ministry and the casual manner in which the family life of the people of God is condemned as ineffective and a mere reflection of a sick culture, I shudder. Then I realize that there are parishes by the thousands where a death grip of institutional cancer proclaims that "The church is an Edsel."

Yet how easy it is to condemn! When the cries for change are only empty echoes and the Lord's Day dawns, people will come with broken hearts and shattered lives and wait for a word to lift and inspire. Then the work of worship will be done, and, by the power of the living God, it will get around all of the hangups men create. In the congregation of broken people the Word is proclaimed and God's love in Christ declared. Not underground, or behind a tree, or in a discussion group but in the congregation. Broken lives will be healed because Christ is prepared to circumvent the pettiness of men. Of course the structures with which we operate in the institutional church are frustratingly archaic and unbelievably tied up in constitutional tangles and the power struggles of little men. Yet those who receive Christ and who respond willingly to his promises and demands are still about the ordinary, daily doing of the Gospel. This is so often neglected by those who are busy either clamoring for change or defending the *status quo,* that what is essential becomes tragically sidetracked.

When we worship we should reflect on what we have long taken for granted: a place of worship, warm, clean and prepared for us; bulletins listing the parish program for the days ahead; all of the participants in the service well-schooled in what is to take place and in their part in it; church school teachers, materials and rooms ready, and the entire parish ready to receive us so that growth in Christ may take place. This clearly means that a great many people are involved in what is regarded as the little things, the leftovers that are painfully routine but are so important if we are to share in worship that will give glory to the Lord.

What about your congregation, your attitude, your willingness to receive, and your joy in believing? There are those who seemingly arrive for worship with unprepared hearts and cluttered minds; others who stalk in with chips on their shoulders, and still others who, with fear and uncertainty, wonder if there really is a clear word for them. At the heart of it all is Christ who came, not to be served but to serve, who was willing to wash his disciples' feet and who showed them the way to doing the job at hand—not sidestepping the menial and the uncomfortable, but seeing the beauty in doing any job well for them.

What does leaving someone else to do the work have to do with the feeding of the five thousand? According to our text, there was only one in the whole crowd who had prepared for the practical necessity of eating.

> One of his disciples, Andrew, Simon Peter's brother, said to him, "There is a lad here who has five barley loaves and two fish; but what are they among so many?" (John 6:8, 9).

We don't read that the lad offered his lunch, but perhaps he did. We also learn a truth that needs emphasis: God is able to do a lot with what we regard as very little. "There is a lad here—but what are [these few loaves and fish] among so many?" What indeed! What does the church, in the midst of the complex structures of our rapidly changing society, have to offer so many who are in desperate need? When the light of Christ lightens the life of a man, and the meaning of being truly healed and truly human is realized, the answer to this question is clear: God is able to do a lot with what we regard as very little.

It is time that we stop discussing the mission of the church and become missionaries. It is time that we stop debating the niceties of ecclesiastical structure and begin ministering to the world around us. It is time that we stop mumbling about what is going to happen in the future and live in the Kingdom of Grace here and now.

This means more than words. It means the recognition of God's multiplication of the fruits of redemption and grace and growth in our lives. Not for a moment can we believe this happens without our complete commitment and involvement. It happens when lives are changed, when preparation is made, when attitudes take on the kind of direction that leads to strength and sharing.

There are wonderful stories of what happens to people who have offered, not loaves and fishes but their lives, their very selves. It does not happen to all in the same way or with the same result, but it can happen to every one of us and, what is more, it should. God does not want us to live on leftovers. He wants us to know that he can take us just as we are and do a lot with what we regard as very little. The feeding of the multitude is the only miracle which is recorded in all four Gospels. Like the disciples, the church is always testing and, like the disciples, Jesus knows what we are and what we can do.

As you have read this chapter, I am certain that you have sensed that you often feel like the boy whose seemingly simple gifts Jesus took and multiplied so mightily. You feel you have untapped resources, and you have. Jesus

Christ is ready to take and use and multiply them, if you are willing to let him, and prepared to let yourself go.

All who read this chapter—a boy here, a man there, a woman, a girl—are resources Christ is ready to tap and use. Only when we see the Holy Spirit filling the lives of the apostles of today will we understand what Christ is ready and able to do through us. There is something elusive about this, as a remark attributed to Karl Barth notes:

> The Church is the place where man searches for God;
> it is also the last place where man hides from God.*

And we do hide, and in hiding we miss the fun and make the Spirit's persuasive task even more ticklish.

Jesus fed the crowd. He did not say piously, "I hope you are not too hungry and that you will get home all right."

Much effort is lost because it is scattered. While it may be stretching things, it seems to me that our Lord would have us know that, in his eyes, even our fragments are important.

But we must carefully distinguish between fragments and leftovers. The miracle was that our Lord fed those who came to hear him, and they were so pleased at the amount of food that they became careless. Jesus still is the Lord who cares for his children. For the first time in history, man has the technical know-how to feed the world's hungry. To be sure, there is no easy answer to either the population explosion or to poverty; nor is there an easy answer to our Lord's multiplying of the loaves and the fishes. There really is no explanation for what hap-

---

*Quoted in *Bittersweet Grace,* Walter D. Wagoner, ed. (New York: The World Publishing Co., 1967), p. 85.

pened after the leftovers were gathered—all twelve baskets.

Jesus Christ did not suffer and die and rise again on the third day in order to form a discussion group or a community of the hungry and lost. When he came to bring abundant life, this meant life in all of its completeness. This is what Paul was talking about when he said, "In him all things hang together." Frightened and fragmented people are always crying for help. And what this text says to you and to me is that, as Christians, we are to be ready to listen and to share ourselves and our possessions so that others may find their cries for help answered.

Clearly, this means preparation for Christian caring and sharing in Jesus' name. This means a change of heart and attitude so that the fragments of our lives can be picked up and cemented together with the honesty that comes from recognizing our dependence on God for all we have, all we are, all we ever hope to be.

When I stood at the window of the hospital nursery with a new father not long ago, he turned to me, his eyes bright with tears of joy, and exclaimed, "Pastor, I'm so grateful, so filled up with love I could burst." This kind of fragmenting, it seems to me, is what is important. Abundant, overflowing, genuine, generous love and concern for others shows itself in the small, ordinary things that often are taken for granted; it shows in not leaving ordinary, daily duties at the doorstep of others; it does not preen or parade but "does"; it realizes that God is able to multiply on a scale beyond our wildest dreams, and it sees life through the eyes of the wholeness of joyous love, not through the fragmentation of selfishness.

As the Word of God enters your life, are you prepared?

What is your attitude? Will this message of what God wants to do for others through you make a difference in the weeks ahead in obvious ways? In your responsibilities as a father or mother, son, daughter, friend, worker, student, will your attitude and preparation, your spirit, acceptance, and willingness be different? When you prepare for worship, when you fill your offering envelope will it be with a fresh sense of joy and an increased cheerfulness in giving, in sharing in the spread of the Gospel? As you take your place in the pew and bow your head for a moment of prayer, will there be a whole group of people on your mental screen to whom you will want to be grateful because of the way God has used them to enrich your life?

It is not enough to go to church, to sit and receive, and to leave. Your gifts are to be used, to be multiplied and shared to bring Christ to men, to build up the church, and to give glory to his name. Because Christ has showered us with his gifts, what you do with his Gospel is important for others as well as for you. Can we pray that we may say of our parish that not only are all prepared, but that all also are involved in sharing in willing obedience to Christ?

For to this you have been called, because Christ also suffered for you, leaving you an example, that you should follow in his steps. He committed no sin; no guile was found on his lips. When he was reviled, he did not revile in return; when he suffered, he did not threaten; but he trusted to him who judges justly. He himself bore our sins in his body on the tree, that we might die to sin and live to righteousness. By his wounds you have been healed. For you were straying like sheep, but have now returned to the Shepherd and Guardian of your souls.

1 Peter 21-25

Chapter Seven

The resilient grace of Christ
takes us from - - -

Old Paths into New Directions

*. . . because Christ himself suffered for you and left you
an example, so that you would follow in his steps.* 1 Peter
2:21 (TEV).

In Charles Dickens' novel *Bleak House* we meet a
fascinating character named Mrs. Jellyby who is incidental
to the story but who nevertheless has made an indelible
mark upon me, just as we are all often marked by seemingly incidental things. With his incomparable manner of
painting a person in words, Dickens caricatures Mrs. Jellyby as the completely misguided zealot. Her passion is
Africa and the plight of the natives there. Her own family
is in chaos; on her table are the remains of poorly prepared
meals; the clutter of months of neglect clogs the rooms of
her house. But she is passionately committed to the salvation of Africa.

Mail arrives in mountains, and her teen-age daughter is
little more than an ink blot as she takes high-blown dicta-

tion about the latest needs of the African situation. From the depth of her own deepest needs, the daughter blurts out to one who has befriended her, "I wish Africa were dead!"

A good cause, the salvation of Africa, but Mrs. Jellyby and those who resemble her have gone a far reach from following in Jesus' steps. Lent is a time for learning to follow Jesus, not in the fragmented frustration that comes from commitment to unreachable goals but in the joy and hope that is born of the little things in life.

In New Guinea, at the beginning of World War II, the United States and its Allies began to fly supplies into one of the most primitive areas of the world. With all of the skills of technological man, the Seabees and others arrived to build roads, airstrips, supply dumps, and barracks. On the sidelines sat the native population. When all was completed, they watched as cargo plane after cargo plane arrived from the sky and disgorged an amazing array of good things. Food, clothing, supplies of all kinds, as well as the tools of military destruction, were brought in from the sky. Never had the natives heard of such a miracle. A new religion was born. After the soldiers and sailors left and the jungle began to reclaim what had been torn out for the purposes of war, the native population built replicas of the cargo planes. Priests of the new religion told the people that the gods of the sky would return if the worship was proper and that, again, the planes would unload untold riches from above. Even now they wait, and the cargo cult has its worshipers.

Isn't it sad, we cluck, that they are so naive that they believe there can be any benefit in following a patently phony faith. There have been Christian missionaries there for more than a hundred years. There must be something wrong if, after all this time, the natives can be taken in by such bunk. What new directions have those missionaries been offering in place of the old ways?

It is late at night after a hard day, and the phone rings at the parsonage. "Listen," says a voice, "what business do you have telling people who don't worship or take communion that it would be a good idea if they admitted they had no concern for Christ or his church and quit pretending to be Christian? Let me tell you a thing or two about the way it was when things were rough. Then we sacrificed for the church and the church wouldn't have been able to get along without us. All of that stuff about worship and prayer and Bible study is fine when you are feeling good and when you have plenty of time, but when things were needed, then we did what was important. We saved the church." Saved the church! Has such insufferable, colossal arrogance ever been uttered by anyone?

Mrs. Jellyby in nineteenth century England, the cargo cult in New Guinea, and the misguided church member in America present great similarities. All are plunging down peculiar paths; all have chosen their models for faith and life; all are unable to sleep secure in selfishness, and all are missing the joy of the new directions Christ offers. We all fit one or a combination of these three descriptions: passionately concerned, to the neglect of those who need us most; sitting around waiting for something to arrive that will radically change our way of life, or hostile and defensive because of our neglect. We plow deep in the ruts of the old paths and new directions pass us by.

Christ left us an example, said the Apostle Peter, so that we would follow in his steps. Are you following him?

To follow in Jesus' steps, it is necessary to know what his example is, and it is my observation that there is little awareness of this and even less interest in following it. Isn't it here that much of the confusion over what it means to be a Christian comes into focus? Following Jesus' example does not mean wearing a flowing robe, long hair, sandals, moving to Nazareth, or becoming a carpenter. It does mean that the good news of the Gospel which retrieves our lives from despair and destruction must be heard, accepted, understood, and shared. It is here that the difficulty begins.

Christ left us an example to follow. Sounds simple, doesn't it? But if I were to ask you how to go about the business of following him, of walking in his steps, of healing your relationship not only to him but to those closest to you, of sharing his good news with others, what would you answer? How would you demonstrate *your* new direction?

Somewhere I read that Noel Coward has a trail leading to his hilltop hideaway in Jamaica that is little more than a goat path. His purpose is to make getting to his home as difficult as possible, and to discourage visitors from seeing him at all. A successful and famous person, he has no need to clear a path for droves of people to come knocking at his door. So he does his best to keep visitors away, except for those whom he invites.

How like him we are. Rather than cutting the ribbon on a four-lane highway to friendship, we raise the barricades and clutter the entrances to our lives until not even a goat path remains. Look around you the next time you go to church. How long has it been since you had some words in haste or anger with another member who now sits on the other side of the church and keeps a safe distance.

Do you sometimes feel that what should be a happy time of thanksgiving is sometimes a time of irritation, such as when the offering plate comes by? When the church service is over, what will your expression, your conversation, reveal of how you are following in his steps? Does the reassuring Word so fill your mind and heart that old ways can be changed and new directions discovered?

My wife and I once were driving across western South Dakota to a meeting. It was late at night, bitterly cold, the snow was blowing, and there was not another car on the road. To save time I decided to take a shortcut by using some side roads. As we traveled, the roads became narrower, less clearly marked and rougher, until finally the road just ran out; it simply disappeared. Obviously, my direction had been wrong; it had led to a dead end.

Many people, church members included, find themselves at a dead end in life, with barriers thrown up through the years. It can be difficult to find fresh, new directions. Beset by aimlessness, we embark upon the dry and empty route of unmarked days which we always hope will be broken by a shortcut to joy and useful involvement. Finally, we must all realize that there is no way to new direction other than to follow the path, the steps, the example of Christ. Knowing this, Peter exclaimed, "Have your minds ready for action."

When Marcus Barth wrote of the church in America,

he titled his book *Fire on the Earth.* In it he described how the churches looked to one who saw them from the outside. His descriptions were devastating in their honesty and depth. As the fire of man's destruction rolled across the earth, Barth found the churches taking many different positions. He saw the Lutherans as having built a wall around themselves; occasionally, as the fire came nearer, someone would crawl up to the top of the wall, look over, and then hurry back to tell the others how bad things were on the outside.

I submit that Barth knew very little about the strength of either the Christian Gospel or the church. I also submit that there are too many parishes where this description is accurate. Old paths are inviting and we often have taken them because they seem to be wholesome, healing, and necessary. And in many respects they are, but the old paths are not the whole answer to the fragmentation of our lives today. Will Rogers once said, "The schools ain't what they used to be and never was." This applies to the church that always faces the future backward. Clinging to the old can stifle the breakthrough of that which is vital and fresh. Following in the steps of Jesus Christ means having the full and abundant inheritance of the apostles and prophets so that we are not tossed about by the winds of change and confusion. But there is much more to it than clinging to flotsam in a sea of chaos. In following Jesus' example, there are these and other areas that should concern us:

To follow in his steps means to take Jesus seriously.
Start at home or at work, and ask yourself whether or not you take Jesus Christ seriously. Can you talk about him

at home? Are you able to have a devotional life that is both enjoyable and inviting? Do you discover fresh avenues for sharing Christ at home? I am convinced that one reason the organized church has so many conventions, meetings, workshops, conferences, is that those who put them on and those who take part in them thoroughly enjoy the energetic involvement in what often is little more than structured, exaggerated irrelevance, totally unrelated to the places where the people who are attending should be following Christ's example.

What does it mean to take him seriously where you live? Read these verses in Peter's letter, from which our text is taken:

> Throw all your worries on him, for he cares for you (1 Peter 5:7). Above everything love one another earnestly, for love covers over many sins (1 Peter 4:8 TEV).

To take Jesus seriously, to follow his example, to break out into new directions, it is necessary to believe that his love covers your weaknesses and failures, so that your home may be open to renewal through him.

To follow in his steps means to be willing to recognize his authority in all of life.

This means breaking out of the old paths. For all of us this is difficult. Some of us will never break out because of the irrational antipathy to Christ's authority in our lives. Yet, to hear him gladly is to learn of the relationship which will point toward new directions in every area of human experience. It's like the breaking through of the sun on a dull and cloudy day. Barriers to growth and freedom which

have created detours in our lives, obstructions which say
"No Trespassing," "Keep Out," "Beware," "Danger," all
are battered down, as the obscure reasons we have for sepa-
rating ourselves from others are revealed in the bright glow
of his love. Christ is, for the Christian, the only authority
for decisions and actions.

To follow in his steps means to readily obey him.

This means to be faithful, to be a disciplined disciple, to
be enlisted in the fellowship of the apostles, prophets, and
martyrs. It is simpler to interpret for ourselves what it
means to be obedient, but let us begin where we live, work,
play, worship. At home the old patterns are secure. Or are
they? Perhaps this is the place where the roads just run
out and there are no longer clear paths. How do you follow
in Christ's steps at home? In what way is your home a
foretaste of heaven for father, mother, other members of
the family?

To grow in favor with God and man is no easy task, yet
it is one that brings joy and stimulation to the relationships
which are meant to be the solid base for strengthening the
rest of life.

Following in Jesus' steps has become a standard tune-out
for almost any kind of suggestion that something dull needs
doing, or that some pet project needs completing and those
who participate are following in his steps. This can bring
an unhealthy reaction and often should. To follow in his
steps is to act with elements of the infectious, the heroic,
the concerned and the vigorous spirit which makes the
Gospel compelling news. He left an example, not so we
could sit and vegetate but so we could follow him. Follow-

ing Christ gives birth to a spirit of joy and excitement and lively, daring concern for the church as a living, breathing instrument for healing.

Being a part of a parish family is an experience that fills life with a sense of the happiness that being in Christ brings. To follow him is to be about the business of helping good relationships happen, in his name. This means many things. In a church in Boston a pastor saw with new eyes the need for mission work outside of the country. He preached the need to share and reach others. Now, each year on that congregation's annual mission Sunday, more than a quarter of a million dollars is given, over and above an already courageous local budget. Following Christ involves lifting the giving of many out of the straight-jacket of negative obligation into the large arena of positive responsibility. Yet how often our following reflects David Head's tongue-in-cheek prayer:

> Lord, I know it is the task of the church to preach the Gospel. But do we have to cross thousands of miles of sea or sky to do it? Deliver us from straining our eyes to see some special need at the ends of the earth, while ignoring the responsibilities under our noses. Forgive the longsightedness that gets the nearer task out of focus. Provide men and money for all our needs at hand. And don't call my son to be a missionary.*

What is always of great interest to me is that there are those who will pretend to be, as they say, "on fire for missions," and yet will take no part in the outreach of the

---

*David Head, *He Sent Leanness* (a book of prayers for the natural man). New York: Macmillan, 1959, p. 43.

congregation to which they belong. People like this can be found in every congregation, people for whom the black man is an object of deep concern while the black militant in America is an object of distaste. How do we define mission anyway?

> . . . Christ himself left you an example, so that you would follow in his steps (1 Peter 2:21 TEV).

People heard Jesus gladly when he said, "A new covenant I give you, that you love one another." This love was to penetrate the whole of life, bringing to a congregation such willingness to listen, adventure, obey, and accept that the fervor of new life would overflow and others would be ready to follow in Jesus' steps.

This is where we are today. We all need to be ready to answer these questions: Are we following Christ's example? Are we walking in his steps? Make it personal, or the questions are lifeless. Am I? Are you?

What do you think? Is it time that you broke away from your old paths and start in fresh, new directions? To follow in Jesus' steps is to know where your life is heading.

The Lord said to Moses, "Say to Aaron and his sons, Thus you shall bless the people of Israel: you shall say to them,

The Lord bless you and keep you:

The Lord make his face to shine upon you, and be gracious to you:

The Lord lift up his countenance upon you, and give you peace.

"So shall they put my name upon the people of Israel, and I will bless them."

Numbers 6:22-27

Chapter Eight

Tensions are released
as we learn that we have - - -

Aaron's Legacy Writ Large

"The Lord lift up his countenance upon you, and give you peace." Numbers 6:26.

Holy Communion is a benediction, a blessing from God. Sharing in this meal means sharing in a legacy of grace. As we bare our souls before God and prepare to share in the celebration of communion, our thoughts need direction in order that we may receive with joy the gifts God offers. Into our neurotic age of unwholesome tensions, the blessing of Holy Communion comes with compelling power. Here broken lives are remade and the fragments of our rebel hearts put together. It is a legacy *from* God *for* the people of God, and the church seals her children with this blessing of peace and release.

How often have you heard these familiar words of Aaron, the high priest, "The Lord bless you and keep you"? How often have you felt God's presence as you have gone from worship with this benediction filling your mind and heart?

Yet it can become so familiar that, handled carelessly, its power to heal is neglected, overlooked, forgotten. So also with Christ's thanksgiving meal which is meant to be a sacramental benediction in our lives; so also with the time of preparation we call Lent.

"The Lord bless you and keep you . . ."

It is customary for us to bow our heads when the benediction is announced, just as it is the custom among some of us to kneel at the communion rail when we receive the consecrated elements of bread and wine. As the ancient people of Israel were blessed, we also are blessed during communion so that we might, in turn, help others. During Lent, Communion often becomes a sad scene. It could be, must be, the light of Christ bringing his benediction into our broken lives. Lent *can* be a time for release and rejoicing.

We need God's blessing as well as his keeping. As a people, we have been recipients of God's grace in dramatically visible ways. Yet there are many who fail to recognize that all the blessings of this earth come from God alone. In a sense, all of us are living on divine welfare. When we forget this, we exhibit the angry, taut, harried, hurried, easily upset, quickly irritated, and unwholesomely exhausted attitudes which plague our tension-ridden and "thing"-obsessed age. When we forget this, we become fearful and defensive and tied up in knots. So Aaron's legacy needs to be written large across the doorposts of our personal lives. These words from God, "The Lord bless you and keep you," are clear and comforting. Through love in action, we are made aware of the blessing and the keeping of God.

"The Lord make his face to shine upon you and be gracious to you . . ."

Do you remember what happened when Moses came down from Mount Sinai? His face shone so brightly that those who looked at him had to shield their eyes. When Paul wrote to the congregation in Philippi, he said:

> Do everything without complaining or arguing, that you may be innocent and pure, as God's perfect children who live in a world of crooked and mean people. You must shine among them like stars lighting up the day, as you offer them the meaning of life (Philippians 2:14-16 TEV).

In Holy Communion God grants us the grace to unlearn all of the rasping attitudes that make us mean and nasty and small. Here we are summoned, like Moses, to a holy place and should, in reverence and awe, bow low before the purity and grace of God. Here God's face shines, and he is gracious. Without the gift of faith, a fog of unbelief veils the light of the Gospel. It is not enough to hear the words; it is not enough to say they are true; it is essential to trust in the Lord who offers his gifts in life and in death.

A robust man who recently had a heart attack told me that when he lay in the hospital not knowing whether he would live or die, he thought of the casual, flippant way he had regarded Christ and loyalty to his church. He said, "It took a jolt to make me see that you can't be a Christian by degrees. Either you are one all the way, or you are not.

And I know I am a Christian, all the way. Now I know what the benediction is saying." His face and his attitude reflected the grace of God and Christ. What a wonderful source of release, of liberation from the paralysis of doubt and fear. He was alive to the grace of God.

Yet the grace and favor of God is given neither indiscriminately nor accidentally. Look within yourself. Is your spiritual health in balance? When any of us come to awareness of the grace of God, we have learned the fundamental lesson of total dependence upon the Lord. As we come to the Lord's table, the grace of God is shared again. Isn't this reason enough to set aside the season we call Lent?

"The Lord lift up his countenance upon you and give you peace"

While in England recently, I listened to an early morning radio interview with a nineteen-year-old girl who recently had been baptized. Why, she was asked, did she decide that she wanted to become a Christian? Didn't she know that young people are leaving the church in droves? Her answer was given with quiet sincerity. "God called me through the Word of Christ," she said. "Before I came to know the love of God, I was always anxious and tense. In the church I have discovered what peace means." She went on to tell more of how her life was transformed. It was a deeply moving kind of testimony to the Holy Spirit's power to call others to the living faith.

When God lifts up his countenance upon us, what happens is so all-encompassing that it is difficult to imagine. Randolph Crump Miller wrote that

... the peace that passes understanding offers the clue to the meaning of our existence. We do not exist for food and clothing, for little idolatries and big successes, or even for moral crusades. *In the last analysis, we exist only for God. This is what we fail to accept, and so we burn ourselves out seeking lesser goals.**

Deliverance from the sickness of self-seeking, liberation from the tyranny of petty goals—these are part of what the legacy of faith is all about. Strangely, after years of the continuing grace and care of God, we seem to be more in need of relearning this truth than were Christians of any other era. We asked the wrong questions so long that the benediction of the Gospel has been obscured. Think of such questions as, "What can I get out of going to church?" "What good does being a Christian do me?"

Jesus did not offer the sterile limbo of anonymity in this life. He said:

> Never think that I have come to bring peace upon the earth. No, I have not come to bring peace but a sword! Anyone who puts his love for father or mother above his love for me does not deserve to be mine, and he who loves son or daughter more than me is not worthy of me, and neither is the man who refuses to take up his cross and follow my way. The man who has found his own life will lose it, but the man who has thrown it away *for my sake* will find it (Matthew 10:34, 37-39).

Only when the clinging to old ways is cast away and the freedom born of a partnership in a great cause is realized can the benediction of peace becomes a reality. *The peace of God is not a pious kind of escape mechanism whereby*

---

*Randolph Crump Miller, *Be Not Anxious* (New York: The Seabury Press, 1957), p. 15.

we may hide from the realities of the world around us.
Not at all! The peace of God comes in its fullness as we
learn to lift up our eyes above the confusion around us
and know that Jesus Christ is Lord. This is why G. A.
Studdert-Kennedy could write:

> Peace does not mean the end of all our striving,
> Joy does not mean the drying of all tears;
> Peace is the power that comes to souls arriving
> Up to the light where God Himself appears.
>
> Joy is the wine that God is ever pouring
> Into the hearts of those who strive with Him.
> Light'ning their eyes to vision and adoring,
> Strength'ning their arms to warfare glad and grim.*

Even now we find the Gospel of Jesus Christ a disturb-
ing kind of good news. We cannot buy our way to peace
or acceptance through strain or stress. Fulfillment comes
from placing ourselves entirely and without reservation in
the hands of God. This is what Jesus is talking about when
he said:

> "Peace I leave with you; my peace I give to you;
> not as the world gives do I give to you. Let not your
> hearts be troubled, neither let them be afraid" (John
> 14:27).

Perhaps it would be helpful to look at just what the
legacy of Aaron is, and why we should write it large upon
the days of our lives. *"The Lord bless you"*—the blessing

The Best of G. A. Studdert-Kennedy (New York: Harper & Row, 1948).
Reprinted by permission of the publishers.

comes from God, a gift given, not deserved. *"The Lord be gracious"*—grace is from God freely offered through Jesus Christ. *"The Lord give you peace"*—to calm the spirit and strengthen the soul. Peace is given to complete the gift.

Having received the gift, we are to be a blessing, to be gracious, to bring peace into our homes, our work, our churches, our communities, and the world. This never happens by accident, by making some minor adjustments, by turning over a new leaf. We become living benedictions *only* when selfishness is eliminated from our lives.

God has blessed us; we also are to be a blessing.

This affects our words and conversation, our respect and concern for others, our loyalty to the church and concern for its mission. In all of these we are to be a blessing. Are you?

God is gracious to us; we also are to be gracious.

Just as worry and unresolved anxiety can shorten our lives, so the serenity and maturity of a gracious spirit can add fruitful days to our years. Simple courtesies are the key, and they demand courageous and daring faith. There is no substitute for gracious acceptance in the life of a Christian.

God gives his peace; we also are to share his peace.

When our confidence and strength come from the Lord, and when we seek his kingdom and his righteousness, we will share in the legacy of God which he grants his children.

In our lives, these three gifts are to loom large as we surrender and serve and show clearly the faith, and blessing of the living God.

> The Lord bless you . . .
>> The Lord be gracious to you . . .
>> The Lord give you peace . . .
> In the strong name of Jesus!
>> Amen.